MY [illegible]

"WHAT I DID [illegible] SAW BETWEEN THE 9TH JUNE AND 25TH NOVEMBER, 1857;"

WITH

AN ACCOUNT OF

GENERAL HAVELOCK'S

MARCH FROM

ALLAHABAD TO LUCKNOW

BY

A VOLUNTEER
(W. O. SWANSTON, 7TH MADRAS N.I.)

The Naval & Military Press Ltd

published in association with

FIREPOWER
The Royal Artillery Museum
Woolwich

Published by
The Naval & Military Press Ltd
Unit 10 Ridgewood Industrial Park,
Uckfield, East Sussex,
TN22 5QE England
Tel: +44 (0) 1825 749494
Fax: +44 (0) 1825 765701
www.naval-military-press.com

in association with

FIREPOWER
The Royal Artillery Museum, Woolwich
www.firepower.org.uk

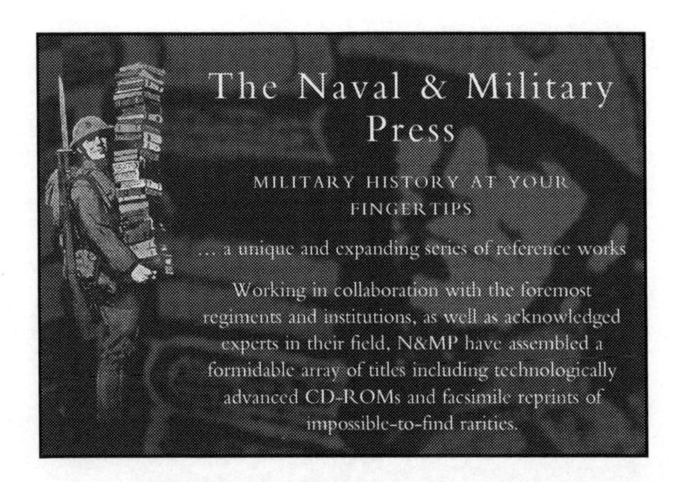

In reprinting in facsimile from the original, any imperfections are inevitably reproduced and the quality may fall short of modern type and cartographic standards.

Printed and bound by Antony Rowe Ltd, Eastbourne

DEDICATED

WITHOUT PERMISSION

TO

THE KINDEST OF FRIENDS, AND ONE OF THE COMPANY'S

BEST AND BRAVEST OFFICERS,

CAPTAIN LOUSADA BARROW,

FIFTH REGIMENT M. L. C.

LATE IN COMMAND OF THE VOLUNTEER CAVALRY WITH HAVELOCK'S FORCE.

PREFACE.

SINCE "my Journal" was written, a long time has elapsed; and had any one told us on the 25th November, 1857, that we should not see the fall of Lucknow till the 16th March 1858, we should have laughed at him: but so it has happened. For three months did General Outram hold his position at Alum Bâgh in the face of a countless army of the rebels, constantly attacked by them, as constantly repulsing their attacks, and now and then himself taking the offensive and driving the enemy back. It was no easy life that his force had there; and, when the history of this Rebellion shall be written in full, the holding of the Alum Bâgh by Major General Outram and his small force will be looked upon in its proper light, and I hope estimated accordingly.

Lucknow has fallen; and the British flag again waves on the Residency. The Volunteer Cavalry has been broken up; the Officers have gone—some to their civil duties, some home, and some elsewhere: the uncovenanted Volunteers have been allowed to go and seek other employment: and that little body of men, which the Right Hon'ble the Governor General was pleased to call "Captain Barrow's devoted band," is become one of the "has beens." Few will ever remember that, at the outbreak of this mutiny, the only Cavalry that General Havelock had, through his march from Allahabad to Lucknow, was a corps called The Volunteer Cavalry, composed at first entirely of Officers and Gentlemen, who served as Privates in the field.

Perhaps I may be wrong, but I do not think the services of this little band have been duly appreciated, at least by His Excellency the Commander-in-Chief. That they were so by the late Major General Sir Henry Havelock we know; and that they are so by Sir James Outram will be seen by the following letter, of which we are all proud, as coming from one of our best Commanders—"the Indian Bayard";—

Lucknow, 29th March, 1858.

MY DEAR BARROW,

We are about to separate, perhaps for ever; but believe me I shall ever retain you in affectionate remembrance, and ever speak with that intense admiration, which I feel, for the glorious Volunteers, whom you have commanded with such distinction. It would afford me much pleasure to shake every one of them by the hand, and tell them how warmly I feel towards them; but this is impossible. My pressing duties will not allow me even to write a few farewell lines to each of your Officers: but I trust to your communicating to them individually my affectionate adieu, and sincerest wishes for their prosperity. May God bless you and them!

Ever your sincerely attached friend,

J. OUTRAM.

TO CAPT. BARROW, *late Commg.*
Volunteers.

"MY JOURNAL."

NOTE.—"MY JOURNAL" was not written with any intention of publication. It consists merely of a few rough notes kept by me for the benefit of one, from whom I was necessarily separated during these troublesome times, and to whom I knew an account of my doings, though ever so short, would be acceptable. But several of my friends have persuaded me that, as hitherto no account of Havelock's extraordinary advance to the relief of our beleagured brethren in Lucknow has been published, my narrative, though rather meagre, would be acceptable to the Public. Trusting therefore chiefly to the interest of the subject, I put it into the hands of the printer.

ON the 9th of June, 1857, I had left the Salone *kacheri* (where every thing had been going on much as usual, with this exception that the crowd of suitors had for several days gradually decreased) about 3½ P. M. for a few moments, when, just as I reached Capt. Barrow's (Deputy Commissioner) gate on my return, I met Capt. Thompson (Commanding 1st Oudh Irregular Infantry at the station) talking to a Sowar,* who appeared to have just come off a journey. On asking what was the matter, he said, that he had just escaped from a party of the mutineers from Allahabad,† consisting of a wing of Infantry, two

* About sixty men of the third Oudh Irregular Cavalry had been sent from Lucknow to Salone to strengthen us, as it was the general opinion that the Irregular Cavalry would stand firm, after the Infantry had gone. How much we have all been deceived has been shewn by the issue.

† The first intimation we had of the outbreak at Allahabad was from one of our Thannadars, who reported that he had secured two or three of the prisoners from the Allahabad jail, who had escaped, and brought the news that the Regiment stationed there had mutinied and released all the prisoners, and that all the Europeans had taken refuge in the fort.

troops of Cavalry, and two guns; that they were marching on to Salone, and were then within five miles. This looked rather too close to be pleasant; so we took the man down to *kacheri* to Capt. Barrow, where, after again interrogating him, we decided it was time to prepare for the reception of any mutineers who might come. We therefore left *kacheri:* Capt. Thompson turned out his Regiment, and, loading two old guns we had there with grape, he stood ready for any thing that might occur. We on our part turned out what was then called the new levies—about one hundred and fifty men enlisted in our Police, whom we had armed, and were drilling. At the same time we sent out some trustworthy men in the direction the Allahabad mutineers were said to be coming, and also towards Sultanpore, from whence another body of mutineers were said to be marching on us. We waited in this state of readiness for about an hour, when our spies returned, and reported that the road was clear in both directions, and that there was no sign of any mutineers: so we turned in the Regiment, and, having set guards of the new levies all round Capt. Barrow's house, and placed the lying Sowar in confinement, we went home. The truth was, the mutineers in our own station had thought that by causing an alarm of "They are coming" to be spread, they would make us take suddenly to flight, and so leave them in quiet possession of our treasure, consisting then of some 500,000 Rs. But when they found that their plan did not answer, they had recourse to another, viz. open mutiny.

It must be remembered that at this time the Regiments at Lucknow had mutinied; Fyzabad, and Sultanpore were (as the expression then was) "gone," and Futteypore likewise; at Allahabad all the Europeans had retired into the Fort, the native Regiment (6th B. N. I.) having mutinied; that the whole country was up in arms, and Cawnpore in a state of siege. We were therefore quite surrounded by mutineers: all the dawks (except that direct to Lucknow, which we managed to keep open) were closed, and every road of escape seemed to be shut against us : but we never lost heart. We hoped, almost against hope, that we should be able still to weather the storm (and if we did, what an honor !), and we put our trust in Him, who had hitherto kept us in peace and quietness. We all dined together at Capt. Barrow's that evening; and, with the exception of Capt. Thompson and Lieut. Chalmers, who slept in the lines with their men, we slept at Capt. Barrow's also—thinking that if any thing did take place we ought to be together, and as near the only lady (Mrs. B.) as possible. The night passed off quietly enough, but the next morning shewed us we had not much longer to remain. The sepoys of the Regiment were all moving about the place armed and accoutred, and were sending their luggage out of the place; and about six o'clock Thompson came and told us, he could do no more, for his men were in open mutiny. We had a long consultation, and determined that we had remained at our post as long as we could, and that we had nothing left but to provide for our own safety. While we were consulting together, one of our most influential Talookdars, Hunnowant Sing, came in and informed us, that the game was up (which we knew before), and that we must go that day, or we might be sacrificed; that, if we could leave at about 4 P. M., he would meet us about a mile out of the Station with some of his men, and conduct us to one of his Forts, where for the present we should be safe. This we agreed to do; and he left us to make preparations.

I may here mention, that this man Hunnowant Sing, in accordance with the policy brought into play at the annexation, had been deprived of the greater part of his estate, which was in the King of Oudh's time very valuable, had consequently been reduced from a very wealthy and influential position to quite the contrary, and had even, under instructions from the authorities, been confined in our jail for not paying up part of his revenue. Notwithstanding all this, he had, I think, a personal friendship for Capt. Barrow, for he was a quick enough man, and saw that Barrow was acting up to orders, and much against his own judgment. It was in a great measure to this friendship that I attribute Hunnowant's conduct, though the old man may have had an eye on the future when he thus acted; for he all along believed that we should be back in Oudh some day. Had our annexation policy been different, I think we should have had many friends where we had enemies. We hoped to make friends of the new men we raised up, but found, to our cost, that in the time of need they were wanting. The truth was they were not strong enough to hold their own, much less to assist us; though I believe many, for their own sakes, would have done so if they could.

At about eleven o'clock, Thompson came and told us that his native officers had come to him, and promised faithfully that, if he would give the whole Regiment six months' pay out of the Treasury, they would march with us, colours and all, to Allahabad. At first, we would not hear of such a thing, it seemed so like bribing our own servants to remain faithful: but when we considered the matter again—that the Treasury was in the hands of the mutineers, who could help themselves without any asking, and that if, by giving six months' pay we could save the rest of the Treasure and the Regiment, it would be worth doing so—we determined on trying it. The Regiment had no sooner received the money than we found upon what a reed we had been leaning. The guard at the jail left, and all our prisoners escaped; the men became more sullen than ever; and (what was worse than all) the detachment of Harding's Cavalry now came and claimed six months' pay, the same as the Infantry had received; and, after them, our Police would doubtless have come. We had made a false move, and were suffering from it: but our position was such it was very difficult to know how to act. We determined to pay up all our establishments, and then quit. I had been down to the Treasury for money two or three times that day, and, thinking that perhaps the guard over the Treasure might not like me to take any more, I took one of the native officers down with me to shew the guard, that *it was by permission of those then commanding* that I was drawing the money. When I arrived at the Treasury, the sentry called for the Jemadar on duty, who came and at once permitted me to open the cash chest; when he saw the other native officer with me, he asked why he had come, and, on being informed, turned to me with tears in his eyes, and asked if he had ever hesitated in permitting me to take money. I tried to explain it away, but did not succeed very well: the old fellow seemed really hurt—and yet he was a mutineer and a rebel at heart.

As soon as we paid our people, they immediately all forsook us; our police, who had sworn to stand by us, leaving us also, and among the first a man whom I had got promoted to be a Jemadar, and who an hour before had with tears in his eyes sworn to stick to me through thick and thin. At about 4 P. M. we prepared to start, Mrs. B. and two children in Carnegie's Buggy, and the Apothecary's wife and his family in another Buggy: the Sergeant Major (who had been very ill) with his wife and family were to go in Barrow's bullock coach, and we men on horseback. Our party was seventeen in number, nine of whom were women and children. We started, *all* our servants having forsaken us, except Capt. Barrow's three Madrassies, with the clothes on our backs and our swords by our sides, not knowing how long we might have to live, as now, that we were obliged to go, every man's hand was against us. We had some twenty-four of our new levies, about the same number of new jail Burkundazes, and one Jemadar, one Havildar and five Sepoys of Capt. Thompson's Regiment with us—and this was all out of thousands, who a week before would have followed us cringing and bowing to the ground! We had to go right through the Regimental lines, which of course was a rather dangerous thing to do: but as it could not be avoided, we put a bold face on it, and went straight through them. The men were standing armed and accoutred in groups, looking very sulky; the two guns were drawn up, so as to sweep the road we must go, and the men were standing with lighted port-fires in their hands. This was probably for show, and done with the idea of frightening us; but I do not think it made any of our hearts beat faster by one stroke.

About a mile out of Cantonments we were met by our old friend Hunnowant Sing, with about 200 as funny looking a set of men, as could be well imagined; and, after a long ride of about fourteen miles, we arrived about 1 o'clock at night at Dharoopore, where our kind host gave us a hearty welcome and made us as comfortable as he could for the night. Thus ended the memorable 10th of June 1857, the 6th anniversary of my wedding day, to which auspicious event I attribute our having escaped so easily:—but, joking apart, we had very much to be thankful for: we had *all* escaped with our lives from Salone, and I think, with one or two exceptions, we were the only body so fortunate. At Sultanpore, thirty-seven miles off, the Deputy Commissioner and his Assistant had been killed, also the officer commanding and the 2nd in command of the Regular Cavalry corps (15th). At Fyzabad the Commissioner and nearly all the officers of the 22nd native Infantry, the officer commanding the artillery and the Adjutant of the 6th Oudh N. I. had been murdered. At Lucknow three had been killed. Cawnpore was in a state of siege, the end of which is too well known. At Futtehpore opposite to us on the other side of the Ganges, the Judge, Mr. Tucker, had been killed. At Allahabad some eighteen or twenty had been killed, and the remaining Europeans had been shut up in the fort: but we had escaped, and were now in the hands of a man, who had given us his "Bhân," the most solemn oath a Hindoo can take, to see us safe to Allahabad, or any other place, which the Europeans still held. He was, however, a native, on whose most solemn oath we could hardly depend, if Allahabad fell. The natives had all an idea that our rule was at an end; and although our host, who was clever enough, did not, I think, really believe as much himself, still he was evidently playing a double game, trying to keep friends with the Rebels, and still to preserve us from harm—a difficult game to play, but one which he carried through very well, and though he has been, and is now, fighting against us, still I should be very glad to see him forgiven, and shake him by the hand again. Next morning we heard that C. was at Kalikunker, another of our host's Forts, on the banks of the Ganges, where he had taken refuge, after having been robbed of every thing he had by the Thannadar and Police at Manik-pore. This Thanandar had been appointed by C. himself. I forgot to mention that on the night of our arrival here, Hunnawant Sing's son had gone to Alladgunj, where one of our Tahsilees was, and had not only rescued the Tahsildar who was in danger, but had brought in with him all the money then at the Tahsilee, viz. Rs. 12,000, which he gave over to Capt. Barrow, and which he took with us into Allahabad, and delivered to us there before leaving us. Immediately our host heard of C.'s position he sent him down money, told his servants to take care of him, and the next day started off himself to bring him to us. He left at about 4 P. M. on the 14th, and returned with C. and his cousin, who was with him on the night of the 15th. We, as we have mentioned, all left with nothing but the clothes on our backs. Mrs. B. had brought a small supply of wine and beer, some forks and spoons, and had a regular little kit in a cowry basket, which, however, never reached us—the cooly carrying it having bolted. The day after we got to the Fort, the bullock coach which had been left behind was brought in by Capt. B.'s Afghan servant and in it were some few things for Mrs. B. and her children. It was good fun seeing us sitting down to our meals, our dinner consisting of fowls, lamb, curry and rice, dal and chapaties, placed in earthen chatties, or rather earthen saucers, and put on a charpoy, round which on the ground we all sat. I think we each had a spoon, but there was only one knife—so we had to use our fingers pretty well: but we got on famously. Old Hunnowant kept up our supplies, and, as far as we could be, we were very comfortable. It was very hot in the day-time, and what we all felt extremely was the want of employment, as we had come away without any books. We were badly off for clothes of course, but here again our old friend came to the rescue, got us cloth and durzees; and we soon turned out as regular natives. About the fourth day of our being in the Fort, a man, named Chand Khan, came up where we were, and commenced making enquiries about a horse that he said had been lost by Lieut. Grant's party from Sultanpore. After having made his inquiry, instead of going away he remained hovering about in a mysterious manner; at last he came up to Capt. Barrow, and put a letter into his hand, which proved to be from Grant, who (with some twenty-nine most of whom were women and children) had escaped from Sultanpore, and was then under the protection of an old man, named Ajeet Sing, who was not very powerful, though very willing to do all he could. It appeared that this party, from there being so many women and children, and their protector being not very powerful, were really in danger, and altogether in a sad plight; so we, after talking the matter over, we determined to trust our host, and see if he could and would do anything for them. He at once set to work, wrote to a relation of his own, whose *illâká* was in that direction, and also to Goolab Sing, and took their "Bhân" from them for the safety of the party. Grant eventually reached Allahabad with the whole of his party in safety under the escort of his host alone.

About this time all our jail Burkundazes and sixteen of our new levies, who had followed us, asked permission to go to their homes: so we allowed them;—we had now only eight of these men and seven of Capt. Thompson's with us. We lived in an upper story of the house, and used to walk on the roof, when not too hot, and, when up there, very often people came for the purpose of looking at us, as if we were wild beasts. This became so unpleasant that we were obliged to ask our host to put a stop to it, which he did at once by placing a couple of sentries at the stair-case leading up: but, before this was done, a man had been up, carrying in his waistband a very nice duelling pistol, evidently the property of some English Officer. On interrogating him, he told us that he was a Jemadar of Police under Capt. Thurburn, who had given him this pistol; that the Regt.

at Fyzabad had mutinied and all the officers had escaped in boats, and that the civil officers with their families had taken refuge in Raja Maun Singh's Fort, where they then were. We immediately wrote to them, and, promising the Jemadar a present if he delivered the letter, persuaded him to start for that purpose: about four days afterwards he returned with a long story that they had left. This at the time we did not believe, for there was something in the man's manner not straightforward, and we imagined he had never gone. I now think that his story was so far true that he knew they had left Maun Singh's the first time he came to us, but had concealed it for some purpose; and, when the reward was offered him, he determined to absent himself for a few days, and then bring us the right tale, which he might have told us at first—namely, that this party had gone to Maun Sing's, and, after remaining there three or four days, had been sent by him down the river in boats. Eventually after much suffering they arrived at Dinapore in safety.

We now became rather anxious about ourselves: we had been upwards of a week in the Fort, and could gain no information of what was going on at Allahabad. We heard reports of large forces of Europeans arriving daily, which kept us in good spirits; but we could not manage to get a letter conveyed there for us, and although our host continued his attentions, still we began to fancy he was throwing obstacles in our way on purpose. At last two men of our new levies came and said that they would try to get into Allahabad with a letter: so we promised them a large reward if they succeeded, and they started. While they were absent, our friend Chând Khân again made his appearance, with a letter from the Collector of Allahabad, and one from Grant, who with his party had arrived there safely. So at last we found out what was going on, and that the road was quite safe. We then sent for our host's son, he himself having gone on some excuse or other to his other fort, told him the news we had heard, and insisted on leaving as soon as possible. He replied that he could do nothing without his father, but that he would send off a messenger immediately for him. This he did; and next evening the old gentleman made his appearance, and, after a good deal of talking, promised to collect a number of men to escort us, and to start on the third day from that time, as that was a lucky day. Well! we did not like to push him too hard; so we consented. Next day our two messengers, dressed as fakeers, returned with a letter from Allahabad, and they were again sent off to tell Court* when we were to start, so that he might have boats ready for us at the ferry, the bridge of boats having been destroyed. On the day decided on, we left the Fort at about 5½ P. M.—all the women and children in doolies and we on horseback. We had a large escort of our host's followers, and, after a tiresome ride of about twenty miles, arrived at Dhunnâwâ, a small fortress belonging to Shudat Singh, a small landholder in our district. We reached this at about 2 o'clock A. M. and had to lie down outside the fort under a tree, as the owner would not, or really could not, receive us inside. Next morning we went to look at the house, to see if we could not get some accommodation in it, but found it in such a state of dirt and ruin that we preferred to remain under a large banyan tree just inside the walls, under which Shudat Singh, pitched a small tent for Mrs. B. and the children, so that we got on pretty well on the whole; we were well supplied with eatables and milk by our host. Our old host, Hunnowant Singh, on being consulted as to our future movements, told us, that we must pass through the estate of a man (whose name I now forget) who was not favourably inclined towards the English, and that it would be necessary to take his "Bhâñ," and that he should have to go himself for that purpose, which would cause a delay of some hours, so that we would not be able to start before 12 at night.

There were two roads for us to go, one about twelve miles to the Pâpâmow ghât, and the other about twenty miles to the bridge of boats: we wished of course to go the shortest road; but Hunnowant was so decided about taking us the other route, that we were obliged to give in; and he left us to get the Bhâñ from

* The Collector of Allahabad.

the man he had spoken about. He returned at 12 at night, but had now altered his mind about the road we were to take; so that we went the short road after all. As the old gentleman wanted something to eat after his long ride, we did not get off much before 2 o'clock in the morning, and just at daylight we came in sight of the river Ganges, where we met two men, with a note from Court, telling us not to go to the bridge of boats, as that road was not safe, and that he had boats and carriages ready for us at the Pâpâmow ghât: so on we went rejoicing to get so near the end of our troubles.

We arrived at the river, put the horses and ourselves on board the different boats, and wished our kind host a hearty farewell telling him, that ere long we should be back at our old station, when we should not forget his devoted kindness. I must here mention that we could not persuade our old friend himself to cross the river with us, or to allow any of his followers to do so. They had an idea that whoever once got into Allahabad, did not get out again, except as a Christian.

When we offered him some pecuniary reward for all he had done for us, he decidedly refused to accept it; nor would he allow any of his men to take any, although we offered him Rs. 5,000 to divide amongst them. "No," he said, "he wanted no reward then: he only wished us to remember him, when we again got into power; and as for his followers, they were his servants, and were paid for doing as he told them:"—and so we parted. May he get his reward! More than one heart blesses him, for having saved our lives; for there is no doubt that, had he not come forward, we should have found great difficulty in getting to Allahabad, as every man's hand, even those of our own Police, was turned against us, and we were a small party to fight our way through, with the women and children we had with us. But One, mightier than the mightiest rebel, was with us, and watched over us. He brought us in safety through our enemies. May we never forget His goodness in this, as in all things, and may it be the means of drawing us closer to Him.

We found Col. Neill with the 1st Madras Fusiliers, with about 200 men in possession of the Fort, the Seikhs having been turned out and encamped under the walls. Every house had been nearly ruined, and such a scene of destruction as met our eyes, I suppose never was seen, and I hope never will be again;—all sorts of furniture and clothes lying about, all, or nearly all, perfectly useless, as the mutineers seem to have taken a delight in destroying every thing that belonged to the Europeans: even, the lining of the punkas was all torn out. Daily arrivals of Europeans soon filled the cantonments with white faces; and on the 30th June a small force, consisting of 200 of the Madras Fusiliers, 200 of H.M. 84th, 250 Seikhs of the Ferozepore Regiment, 2 six-pounder guns, and 1 twelve-pounder howitzer, with some 60 sowars of the 13th Irregulars and 3rd Oudh Irregular Cavalry, who were supposed to be staunch, started under the command of Bt. Major Renaud of the Madras Fusiliers towards Cawnpore in the hopes of being in time to relieve our gallant countrymen, who were besieged there by the rebels under the Nânâ. On the 1st July, another party of the Fusiliers, about 100 strong, under Capt. Spurgin left in a Steamer to endeavour to make their way up by the river to co-operate with the land force. On the 26th of June, Brigadier General Havelock, who had been put in command of a moveable column to be collected at Allahabad, arrived with his staff; and, finding the great want of Cavalry, obtained permission from the Government to raise a Regiment to be called the Allahabad Volunteer Cavalry. Capt. Barrow was put in command. He made Lt. Grant of the 3rd M. E. Regiment his adjutant, and gave Lt. Swanston the Quarter Mastership. We got about 18 men to join us, amongst whom were Ensigns Brander, 37th B. N. I. Ramsey, Stuart, and Hare 17th B. N. I. Pearson 27th N. I., Woodgate, 11th N. I. and Cornet Fergusson of the 8th B. L. C. All honor and praise to these boys, who were the first to offer their services to the Government they served. Many of them had never even joined their own corps, and none of them had been more than eighteen months in the service. We had also some eight young men, who had been engaged on the railways, but had of course been now thrown out of employ. Altogether we mustered I think eighteen, when we left Allahabad with General Havelock's force on the 7th of July 1857.

Nothing occurred till the 12th. The whole road was deserted, the villages empty and all in ruins, and every here and there bodies were seen hanging from the branches of trees. These had been executions carried out by Renaud's force. On the night of the 11th we made a forced march, and came up with Renaud's force at about 4 A. M. on the 12th. We then marched on some five miles to a place called Belinda about four miles from Futtehpore, where we intended to encamp, and had commenced pitching our tents, when we were ordered with the Irregular Cavalry to move on towards Futtehpore to reconnoitre, as the General had been informed that some of the mutineers had possession of it, and intended disputing the advance (as they thought) only of Renaud's force; so off we went, and were followed by a company of the Madras Fusiliers with their Enfield rifles. We got within about a mile of Futtehpore, when we saw the enemy collected just outside. So we were told to halt, and Capt. Barrow and the Quarter-Master General rode on ahead to within about a quarter of a mile of where the enemy were. At first they were not perceived; but when they were, bugles sounded, drums beat, and out came a cloud of Cavalry after them; so they galloped back to where we were. We waited for the enemy, but they took good care not to come too close. As we were too few to fight, and had only come to see what was going on, we got the order threes about, and fortunate it was so, for we had not got half a mile off when down came the artillery and opened on us. This was my first experience in real warfare—the first time I had heard balls flying in earnest; and I must say, I did not like it, though outwardly I dare say I looked brave enough, and called to our gallant Volunteers to be steady, (as they were all young at it like myself). I then thought I should never get accustomed to the whiz of a bullet, or the sing of a cannon ball; but

I have learned that art, and can now hear them all about me and not even wink an eye. We retired gracefully, the rebels trying to hit us, but not succeeding, the Cavalry in crowds (or clouds, I believe, is the proper word,) trying to get round us, and cut us off from our people: so we pulled up, and the rifles commenced a little practise on them. They evidently thought they were well out of range, and so they were of old Brown Bess: but when they saw two or three of their saddles emptied at nine hundred yards, they turned and never came within range again: and ever since, as they have improved their acquaintance with the Enfield, they have increased their distance, till now they seldom come within 1200 or 1500 yards.

When the enemy's guns first opened on us, those "faithful gallant Irregulars," the black chivalry of India, tried to bolt, but were stopped by Barrow. I have seen these men now, fighting both for and against us, and on all occasions, I have seen them behave in the most cowardly way one could imagine. I always had an idea that the irregular Cavalry would do any thing, but I now disbelieve it. No doubt they will gallop after men who have been beaten, and are running away like sheep, but in a charge to break the enemy I believe they are useless. At last we got safe back to our camp, and General Havelock turned out the force to meet the enemy. We had altogether about 1,400 Europeans, and 550 natives, 8 six-pounder guns, with 2 twelve-pounder howitzers. These were in the centre, with Infantry on each side, and on the left flank the Volunteer, and on the right the irregular, Cavalry: the enemy had between four and five thousand. Our guns opened and so astonished the enemy, that they soon turned; and we then advanced, took twelve of their guns, among them 1 twenty-four pounder, and 1 twenty-four pound howitzer, and drove them through Futtehpore. Our fire was very good, and to a new hand like myself seemed splendid. General Havelock in his despatch said Capt. Maude's firing perfectly electrified the enemy. After driving the enemy through Futtehpore, we encamped on the other side, and the town was given up to *loot*, and afterwards nearly destroyed. Thus ended my first battle.

On the 14th we marched about twelve miles; and on the 15th, at Aong, a small village about four miles on, we met the enemy again. Here they had entrenched themselves, and stood for some little time; but we soon drove them out, taking two guns. We had a few killed; and amongst the number of the wounded was Bt. Major Renaud, who was hit in the thigh: his leg was amputated, and he eventually died. After we drove them out of this, we advanced about four miles further, and again met the rebels at a bridge over a small river called Pundu. They had two large guns here (which we took) in position, but our gallant 1st M. F. with their rifles advanced in skirmishing order, and regularly silenced their fire with the rifles. Here we encamped for the day. We were now within fifteen miles of Cawnpore, and all anxious to go on and save our unfortunate fellow country women there. We little knew what was then taking place! Next morning we advanced about eight miles, and then halted under a tope of trees, where we remained till the men had got their breakfasts; and then on we went about a mile, when we made a flank movement to the right, so as to come round the enemy, who had, we heard, a number of guns in position to keep us from advancing along the road. As we advanced to the right we came under fire of their guns, which, however, they did not seem able to move; so as each Regiment passed, they received a round shot or shower of grape among them: at last we all passed this, and got right round the enemy's position. They had managed by this time to turn their guns upon us, so we had a little game at long bowls in which the rebels delight so much; but soon we got the order for the general advance. It is impossible for any one to give an account of what has happened to every Regiment in any engagement; but it is much more impossible to give a description of the battle of Cawnpore, opposed as we were, a small band of about 1,500, to as many thousands. Every Regiment had its hands full. The enemy had taken up several different positions, so that as fast as two guns were taken from them, we found two more open on us from another direction. The first guns I saw taken, were two, which were opposed to H. M.'s 78th Highlanders; and the splendid way in which this Regiment rushed up under a heavy fire of grape, and took these guns was the admiration of all. This rush was headed by Lieut. Moorsom of H. M.'s 52nd, who was in the Q. M. General's Department of the force. I do not mean to say that he led the Regiment, for it was led (as it always is) by its own officers; but the cool way in which Moorsom cantered up, waving his wide-awake, must have astonished the natives. Two other guns were taken about the same time in another direction by the 64th. As all these guns were taken, they were spiked, for we could not take them on with us, till our work was done. The consequence was, that the rebels, who regularly swarmed all round us, retook two guns, and were unspiking them, when the Seikhs were sent to retake them, which they did in their usual gallant style. It is impossible to mention every thing that each Regiment did on that day; but all was well and gallantly done. The Volunteer Cavalry were too few to do much; so they were kept to support a company of the Madras Fusiliers, who were on the right of all skirmishing. While thus employed, the Deputy A. A. Genl. Capt. Beatson rode up, and asked Capt. Barrow "what he was doing?" adding "there are the enemy." Of course there was nothing for it then but to go at them. *There they were* certainly in thousands, Infantry and Cavalry, and *here were we* eighteen in number. But as at Balaklava, the order was given, and Englishmen knew their duty, and charge they did, right into the thick of the rebels. But what could eighteen sabres do among so many? What could be done, was done; and then the little band had to pull up, to find their loss to be one killed, one wounded, two horses shot dead, and two wounded. How we escaped so well, God knows. The bullets rained upon us: but He, who had been with us all along, was with us still. We pulled up, as we could not, so few of us, pursue too far from our Infantry. When they came up, each Regiment as it came cheered the little band; and our brave old General, riding to our front, said, "Gentlemen Volunteers! you have done well. I am proud to command you." We all pulled up here, (on the Delhi road) thinking the day was ours, when we suddenly found guns opening upon us again in another direction: these had to be taken at the point of the bayonet, our own gun-bullocks being regularly knocked up with the long march and hard work of the day:—and so it went on till dark, when we could see no longer. We bivouacked as we stood. All our baggage, food, and every thing of that sort, were five miles behind. We had nothing to eat, and a very little dirty water to drink; but we were all so tired, that we were glad to lie down as we were, and sleep with our horses' bridles in our hands. We took in this engagement twelve guns of sizes. I was awoke up during the night by my syce, who had found me out, and having a little flour with him, had mixed it with some water, making a sort of paste, which he could not cook for want of fire: this the poor fellow offered me, but I could not, hungry as I was, eat it.

Next morning at daybreak we were all on the alert to find where the enemy were, but none were to be seen. The rumbling of cart and gun-wheels had been heard by the pickets all night. The truth was our enemy had bolted, and left Cawnpore. About 7½ P. M. a tremendous explosion took place, which turned out to be the magazine, which they had blown up. A small party under the Q. M. General was sent in to reconnoitre: they found the place deserted by the rebels; so, after getting up our baggage, we marched into Cawnpore, and encamped on the *maidan* in front of the Cavalry stables, and not far from the spot where poor Wheeler's force had made their stand.

How intently the thoughts of every one of us were bent on the pleasure of releasing our poor fellow-countrywomen, whom we knew to be in the hands of those wretches, can be more easily imagined than expressed,—and how deep and bitter was the curse hissed through the lips of many a hero that day! Had those cowardly brutes heard the oaths of vengeance sworn, they would have turned white with fear: and, oh, when we came to *see* the place where our poor sisters and their little children had been barbarously murdered, the very blood in our hearts turned cold, and then again boiled up with thoughts of vengeance. I have often thought whether we are right to think of revenge, for we are taught, "Vengeance is mine, I will repay, saith the Lord:" and then I have eased my conscience by thinking that I was an instrument in His hands. If I am wrong, may God forgive me, but it is hard to think of what our unoffending women and children suffered, and not have feelings of revenge rise in one's heart. "Mercy, mercy" cries the Sepoy, when, seeing death certain, he throws away his musket, and pleads with clasped hands. *Cawnpore!* is hissed at him, as the sword goes through his vitals. And is it a wonder? Who could look upon that little enclosed yard, reeking in blood as if 100 bullocks had been killed there—see the long tresses of some once fair lady's hair lying in handfuls—and above all the small mark of the little children's feet, printed with their mothers' blood on the floor—and then look down *that* well upon the naked bodies of our poor countrywomen, evidently only rendered lifeless the day before, and not feel that he would never forget it? No! never shall a Sepoy receive his life at my hands; and had I the power I would never forgive a mutineer. If it took fifty years, I would hang every Sepoy, that was caught. I would make India feel that England would never forgive such insults and such barbarity, as has been heaped upon her daughters.

On the 18th, General Havelock made over forty Infantry men to Barrow for his Cavalry, and ordered us to take all the horses saddles and arms of the Irregular Cavalry, who had behaved so badly, to fit our men out with; which we did, and next day we were sent, thus fitted out, to Bithoor with a small force to take the place (it was the head quarters of the villain Nânâ). We went there and found the place deserted. We took twenty guns a number of camels, elephants, stores, &c. &c. and returned; and from that day, till we re-crossed the Ganges after our first advance on Lucknow, our men never had a day's rest, riding generally (for we had picked up a few hunting saddles) in native saddles with native swords as arms, dressed in any clothes they had. They certainly were a funny looking set of Cavalry; but the way they did their duty was the admiration of the whole force. Sixty Cavalry were about a proportionate number to the 900 Infantry; and, with these we used to go upon long reconnoitering expeditions of twenty miles and more, and the cowardly enemy were afraid to come near us. How easily they might have cut us off we all felt; but God was with us, was fighting for us; and the cries of murdered women and children at Cawnpore were still fresh in His ears. Besides the continual duties of reconnoitering and pickets, the Volunteer Cavalry were constantly called upon to furnish parties for escort duties of all sorts, and now and then to assist the Commissariat Department in procuring bullocks for slaughter. Whenever such a party was required, the order would come for a Serjeant, or Corporal, and party from the Volunteer Cavalry immediately: so the party was mounted and off; and it used to afford us much amusement at first, before we were well known, to see the faces of the officers to whom we had to report ourselves on these occasions—how puzzled they used to appear, when they saw a gentlemanly looking man come up and report himself as Serjeant so and so, with party of Cavalry. I remember one occasion especially, when Capt. Thompson (an officer of seventeen years' service, who had commanded the 1st Oudh Irregular Infantry), who was a Serjeant in the Volunteer Cavalry, had to report himself to some young subaltern commanding the Infantry of the party going out—the perplexed look of the young fellow, feeling convinced that Thompson was a gentleman, and not knowing how to address him: but that wore off, and we were soon known.

On the 22nd we commenced to cross the Ganges in order to relieve Lucknow; the river was running strong, boats were few, and we were in the middle of the rains: it consequently took some time crossing the force over, and those who went first were for some days encamped in a low swampy plain, where cholera soon broke out, and many a brave man laid his bones there. At last all were crossed over, and on the 27th we advanced about five miles to the village of Mungawarrah, situated on the crest of a rise, and commanding the country for some distance in both directions. Here we remained on the 28th, on which day, we, the Volunteer Cavalry, were sent to reconnoitre as far as Busseerutgunge, where the enemy were said to have two guns in position, which we were to have taken—if we could, of course. Busseerutgunge is about fourteen miles from Mungawarrah, a small fortified place. On the road we passed through the large village of Onao, once the head quarters of the Poorwah District in Oudh, where we were received kindly by the villagers, who gave us milk to drink, and lights for our pipes, for which no doubt they suffered afterwards from the rebels. When we got to Busseerutgunge we found the place strongly fortified and guns in position sweeping the road; and, noticing the enemy's Cavalry galloping in swarms round our flanks to try and cut us off, we thought it wisest to retire, which we did and arrived all right at our own camp. Next morning, 29th, the force moved in advance; before we had proceeded two miles, the Volunteer Cavalry as usual leading, we found the enemy in force ahead of us. They had taken possession of the village of Onao, and defended it, as they always do walled places, with determination. Here Lieut. Bogle of the 78th Highlanders received the Victoria Cross. The fire was very severe, and we were detained for some time before we could clear out the village; and only succeeded by burning it over our enemy, who at last left. Lieut. Seton, Madras Fusiliers, Aide-de-camp to General Havelock, was here wounded, and Lieut. Richardson of the same Regiment killed: here also Lieut. Brown, Adjutant of H. M.'s 84th was wounded, and, while having his first wound dressed, received two others, from which I am happy to say he has since recovered. We got through the village, at least the head of the column did, the Volunteer Cavalry this time behind—when "bang, bang" we heard milling again, and "Volunteer Cavalry to the front" was passed from mouth to mouth; and they were not long in getting there you may be sure, notwithstanding one man had a hole shot through his helmet. When we got up, we found our men deploying in a tope of trees, and the enemy in thousands deployed just ahead of us, and pouring in grape and cannister, which came crashing through the trees most unpleasantly, I can assure you. Our guns soon opened, the enemy's gradually ceased; and then there was a general advance, with constant cries for Volunteer Cavalry to go and secure two guns here and two there, till we had taken twenty of their guns, and sent them flying as usual before us. We halted here for two or three hours in the hot sun, each man receiving his tot of rum, and a biscuit: when that was done, the Volunteer Cavalry again were sent on to see where the enemy were. We soon found them in position in Busseerutgunge about five miles off: so back we came, when the whole force advanced for another mile. I was sent out with a few men on the right flank to see what was doing there, and we actually got right behind our foes, and saw in the distance, over their heads, (for they were lying down under mounds of earth, or wherever they could, to get protection) the glitter from the bayonets of our jolly Infantry—the stand-by after all of our glorious army: so we thought it advisable to go back and report, and, by the time we did so, we found the engagement had commenced, and a very pretty game at long bowls going on, which soon ended as usual in the general advance, the retreat of our cowardly foes, and the capture of the village with two guns. We went through the village, and encamped for the night; and next day for a change blew a couple of men away from guns, and hung a third. I think we must have had in this engagement some 25 or 30,000 opposed to our 1200, of whom about 900 were Europeans. When God is with us, who shall be against us?

We remained where we were on the 30th; and on the 31st were ordered to march: but what was our surprise when instead of turning to the right we turned to the left, which took us back again to where we had started from! We retired to Mungawarrah, and encamped again. During the week all our sick and wounded were sent over to Cawnpore; and on the 4th, the Volunteer Cavalry were sent on to reconnoitre again, and returned having found the rebels as before at Busseerutgunge. They were ordered to halt on the road; and the whole force at a moment's notice ordered to strike their tents and march away. When we were all formed upon the road the General had a letter from the Governor General, thanking us for what we had done, read out to us, and then he said "Men, yesterday two guns and a small re-inforcement joined us, and I told them to go from the right down to the left of the line, and in every man they would see a hero. You have heard what the Governor General and Commander-in-Chief have said. I shall have to write to His Excellency again to-morrow: and it depends upon you what I write. To-morrow we meet the rebels again in the field." The order was then given to advance; we marched through Onao and encamped for the night. Food and grog for next day were issued, and we lay down where we could, knowing that we were on the eve of another fight, and hoping that we were really *en route* to Lucknow. Long before day-light we were all formed up; and just as it broke we advanced.

When the Volunteer Cavalry, leading as usual, got close up to Busseerutgunge, the enemy, who were in thousands, opened out with blank ammunition from two small guns they had in position, and commenced yelling and making a tremendous noise,—to frighten us, I suppose. We remained where we were, and the line was formed behind us. On the road were two very ominous looking things in the shape of two twenty-four pounders. Our guns opened; after the first two shots from the 24's, there was dead silence among the enemy; after a couple more, the lines advanced; but the rebels had as usual bolted. While a working party was levelling a wall the enemy had built across the road, we amused ourselves by watching the effects of ome shots from the 24's at a lot of the enemy on our left: among whom was a grandee on an elephant, which latter animal, finding the shot rather too close to be pleasant, bolted off as hard as he could, whether with or against his master's will I know not. We advanced through the village; and here for the first time I saw bodies lying mangled by shot and shell. I shall never forget my feelings, sickness of heart and stomach too, so much so that I almost vomited: but how soon one gets used to these sights!—when we returned through the village, I could look at them without a shudder. We advanced through the village, had a little more play at long bowls, took two guns, and then pulled up to breakfast or tiffin, which ever you like. As we lay on the grass in the hot sun (well I remember it, as I had a most splitting headache) we were as usual talking over advance or no advance: all elated as we were, we would one and all have gladly pushed on: but our gallant old leader thought differently, and we were ordered to retrace our steps. How we all abused him, and what grumbling there was then! But now we have learned to appreciate his generalship, and to feel how judiciously he acted.

The Volunteer Cavalry in the retreat of course had again the post of honor, viz. behind all: so we had to keep up all the stragglers, and see that none of the baggage fell to the rear. When we got about two miles from Busseerutgunge, we came up with an elephant that had thrown its load, consisting of the men's kit, which is generally tied up in small long bundles—an elephant carrying some forty or fifty of them. We pulled up and assisted in reloading the beast, and then set off with it; but we had not gone half a mile, when the brute threw its load again. The way he managed it, was this;—he stood still and lifted two legs on the side off the ground, then the two other legs, and so on till he gave himself the motion of a ship rolling on the sea, till at last the ropes, which tied the bundles on his back, became loose, and the whole thing came to the ground. Well, this was too much of a good thing: we saw if we went on loading in this way, we should never get on; so we each seized a bundle, and putting it in front of us, rode on, leaving a small party to bring the elephant on: and so we arrived—a sort of land transport corps—at our old encampment of Mangawarrah, where we found our pots steaming with grub. Thus ended our second advance and retreat.

How these retrograde movements affected me, I cannot, I am afraid, clearly explain. I always felt a sinking at heart, an utter despondency, not at all pleasant, and at the same time a mixture of anger and rage, at being obliged to turn my back on such cowards as we had to deal with. I know when we were obliged to leave Salone, I could not have spoken to have saved my life. It was not fear. I, never during those times had any other feeling than that we should all get safe out of it; and still I felt so enraged and disgusted at being obliged to fly from our post, that I could really have cried.

On the 9th, a mysterious order came round to send all sick and wounded men over to Cawnpore, and also all spare baggage tents and horses; so all was sent, and as it was generally supposed that we were all to recross the Ganges next day, I was ordered to go and take charge of the horses and baggage, and prepare for the reception of the Regiment. On the morning of the 10th, I went and remained there till the evening of the 11th, expecting the force; when I suddenly heard that it had again advanced towards Busseerutgunge. It was too late for me to follow them very well, and I could not find out what was intended. The officer commanding Cawnpore, General Niell, was perfectly in the dark, and advised me to remain where I was. I felt very much inclined to go, for although I thought it hardly possible, still I imagined they might be going on to Lucknow, and I would not have missed that for any thing; but it was fortunate I did not go, for if I had I should have had a long ride of twenty miles to catch them up, perhaps when the engagement was over, and then to ride back all the way with them again.

The third advance on Busseerutgunge was much the same as the 2nd, and the fight the same as usual, except that the enemy had thrown up a small field-work about two miles on the river-side of Busseerutgunge, from which they poured into us a heavy fire of grape and cannister. The Volunteer Cavalry appear to have had the full benefit of this; though as usual no one was hit, except Young Fergusson, scratched by a piece of a shell. So hot was this fire, and so well directed did it appear to the rest of the force, that, when the affair was over, several men rode up to us, to see who had been knocked over, or rather who had escaped. In this engagement we had 600 Europeans and some 200 Seikhs—no large force to do what they did, viz. lick some 10 or 15,000, and take two guns. Our force returned after the fight to Mungawarrah; and then next day with the assistance of the steamer the whole of them crossed to the Cawnpore side of the river, and were housed in the few houses that remained unburned.

Thus ended our first advance across the Ganges to the relief of our fellowcountrymen in Lucknow. How sick at heart we all felt I leave you to imagine, as we knew reinforcements could not reach us under a month, if so soon; and we were under the impression that the garrison at Lucknow were then on half rations, and could not hold out so long. But what could we do? we left Allahabad 1500 strong, and had received perhaps 400 men more since we left: and we were now reduced to 600 European fighting-men of all arms, fit for duty, or rather who could be spared for duty across the river. As Cawnpore had to be held, we felt it was hopeless to attempt it, in face of the countless hordes we had to meet. Although we were unable to proceed to Lucknow, there is no doubt that we relieved the little garrison very considerably, by drawing a great part of the besieging force away from Lucknow to meet us in the field; and, even when we recrossed the Ganges to Cawnpore, they were obliged to keep a considerable force to watch us: so that, as we afterwards heard when we got to Lucknow, we had actually relieved them in a great measure: and, although it must have been very heart-sickening for them to hear of our retreat, still they knew that friends were near them, and that we should advance again directly we were in a position to do so.

On the 15th August, in the evening, we received an order to be ready to march at four next morning: so we were all immediately on the *qui-vive;* and at the time appointed we took our post where ordered, and found the whole force ready to march, consisting of about 1400 men and fourteen guns, two of which were 24's—a larger battery than we had ever had in the field. We soon found our destination was Bithoor, where the rebels had again taken up a position; and, as it was rather too close to Cawnpore, our gallant old leader determined to drive them out. In this he certainly appeared to know the rebel well. Never let him rest. If you have any force to move with, follow him up; otherwise he immediately fancies you are afraid, and either attacks you in countless numbers, or sets to work with labour to any amount at his disposal, and strengthens himself in some position. He is like a jackall: if you leave him alone, he goes sneaking about, doing all the damage he can: but just gallop after him, making as much noise as you can, and you soon run him down. It was a beautiful day: the country all round was looking nice and green, and it was pleasantly cool with a fresh breeze blowing. As we rode along the hard well made and well known road, we discussed the probability of the rebels making a stand at a bridge about half way, which from its position offered every facility for a good defence: but on, on, we went, our advanced guard and flankers still going quietly on, till we sighted the bridge, came up to it, and passed over it. No! no enemy: they had neglected, as they often did, one of their best chances: but they have done this so often, that one cannot help feeling that our God has blinded their understanding. When we arrived within about a mile of Bithoor, our advanced men gave signs of the enemy at hand, and soon we saw their Cavalry arriving in hundreds on our left flank. When they had pulled up well out of rifle-shot, and had collected together a little, bang bang went a couple of doses of shrapnel into them, and then it was the de'il take the hindermost. Just then a number of them came straight out of Bithoor down the road, as if they were going to indulge in a charge: but seeing the blue *topees* of the dreaded rifles, they too turned tail and bolted. Our line was formed, and on we went; Tytler, and Moorsoom H. M.'s 52nd, rode on in advance to try and find out where the guns were, which they soon enough did, as the rebels opened on them with round shot. This being all they wanted, they returned, and the enemy found out that sniping at single horse-men with nine-pounders is not so easy as it looks. Steadily our line advanced, till we got well within range, when our guns opened, and after a short time we saw the Highlanders tumbling in through the embrasures of a little work the rebels had raised to their left. Two guns were taken. On the extreme of our right, the gallant blue bonnets (1st Madras Fusiliers) got right amongst the enemy with their bayonets, and bayonetted a number of them—the first time we had that pleasure: but they could not follow up their advantage. They were exhausted with the twelve miles march, and the fight after it. Had the Volunteer Cavalry been with them, they might have done something; but they were on the extreme left, watching the Cavalry. The enemy here gave us more trouble than they had ever done before. They had a very strong position, and the fields being at this season high with sugar-cane and grain of different sorts, they found good shelter there, and made use of it accordingly; for a native certainly does know how to fight behind cover. But this as usual ended in our driving the enemy out of their position, and taking their guns. We then advanced through the village, and halted in different topes on the other side.

The Volunteer Cavalry, having thrown out videttes, lay down to await the arrival of their mess-kit, which had left Cawnpore, through some blunder, three or four hours after the force. Suddenly "bang" went the vidette's piece. Two or three of us were soon in our saddles; and there, to our surprise, we saw a native officer and a Havildar of Cavalry in full uniform, looking at us within a hundred yards of us! They looked just as much astonished as we did, but soon got over it, when they saw the rush made at them: but being on better and fresher horses than we were they soon distanced us, and so, giving them a parting shot, we returned. What they had come up so close for I know not, unless they really did not know we were there, as we were quite hidden in the tope; or perhaps it may have been the Quarter Master General of the rebel army come to reconnoitre our position: however we never saw any thing more of him.

We waited, and waited patiently, or perhaps not very patiently, for our mess servants to come up, to get some of our rations cooked; but none came: so we had to do the best we could on biscuit and steaks fried on the embers, and our tots of rum. Hunger is the best sauce, says an old adage; and we certainly did justice to the victuals. A twelve-mile march, with a fight afterwards, does not decrease one's appetite. We remained at Bithoor that night, and returned next morning to Cawnpore. About two miles out of Bithoor, the non-appearance of our mess kit was fully accounted for, by the remains of broken boxes, plates, &c. &c., which we recognized, and also the dead bodies of two or three of our mess servants: poor fellows, they had started late, and had been cut off by the enemy's Cavalry. We arrived in Cawnpore late in the afternoon, and took up our quarters in the houses again, where we remained two or three days; and then were ordered to encamp on the plain in front of Wheeler's entrenchment. For the first day or two all went on well enough; but then it came on to rain, and we soon found ourselves in a regular swamp: nothing would keep the water out of our tents: it seemed to soak up from the ground: and the only thing we could do was to put all our things on the chairs, or tables, and ourselves lie on our beds. This state of things could not last long: cholera broke out, and the men, weakened by exposure and hard work, gave in one by one and died. We were then ordered to leave our tents standing, and take possession of some sheds there, which fortunately sufficed for the whole force. But it was too late: cholera had got among us; and certainly and quickly it did its work. We, the Volunteer Cavalry, lost ten—six of whom died in twenty-four hours; many more had slight attacks and recovered; those whom death had marked as his own, were taken; and then gradually the dire disease left us. We then set up foot-games, and races of different sorts to keep up the men's spirits, and turn their thoughts from the late melancholy events. We of the Volunteer Cavalry set to work to clothe ourselves and the men in something like uniform, and also to get them proper saddles and arms; and by the time General Outram arrived with reinforcements, on the 17th September, (I think it was,) we did look a little respectable, and could move about somewhat in order, and, when we charged, looked rather formidable to the rebels.

On the 17th September, General Outram arrived with the 90th and 5th, some heavy artillery, and some sixty (supposed to be staunch) Cavalry (Native) of the 12th Irregulars under Lieut. Johnson of the Bombay Army. On the 19th, we crossed the river over the bridge of boats, which had been built, under great difficulties, by Captain Crommelin, Bengal Engineers; and, driving the advanced guard of the enemy before us, we encamped behind a ridge of sand, which runs along the banks of the river about half a mile off it. On the 20th, the Volunteer Cavalry were sent to reconnoitre: and that evening the order of march was issued for next day. At day-break on the 21st, the whole force was in readiness, and formed up: after advancing about a mile, we deployed in order of battle, and marched on to the enemy's position. The balls began to fly about as usual; but our line steadily advanced. H. M.'s 5th, on the left, advancing in skirmishing order, soon drove the enemy right back. On we pressed, when down came an Aide-de-camp with "Volunteer Cavalry will advance. Off we went, and soon came up with General Outram, who, riding stick in hand, headed us. Round we went to the right and took the rebels in rear, and then commenced the cutting up in good earnest. The pouring rain soon drenched us, but as it also did the same to the muskets and matchlocks of the enemy, rendering them useless, we were rather thankful for it. Down, down wentthe wretches. "Cawnpore, my lads, remember Cawnpore" was the battle-cry: and woe to the black skin that came under our swords. At least 250 must have been cut up. Our gallant leader, General Outram, not deigning to draw his sword, kept hitting the enemy as he came up to them with his stick, leaving it to those behind him to kill:—and you may be sure they spared no one. Two of the young officers, who had been doing duty with the 6th Native Infantry at Allahabad, and had escaped the massacre, recognized the drill Naik of the Regiment. One of them called him by name. He immediately threw down his musket, turned round with clasped hands, and crying for mercy, said, "Yes, sir!" The only reply he got was two swords through him. Our Serjeant Major Mahony, of the 1st Madras Fusiliers, got badly wounded in taking the Regimental colours of the 1st Bengal Native Infantry from the hands of two men who were defending it: for this he was named for the Victoria Cross, but I am sorry to say he has not lived to receive it: he died of cholera in October at Alum Bagh. We took the whole of the camp of one Regiment, the 1st Bengal Native Infantry, all their drums and pots, &c.; but, being unable to carry them off, we destroyed as much as we could, and then, dashing on again, came up with the enemy in full retreat. We succeeded in taking two large guns, and numbers of camels and carts. There were several elephants, but we could not succeed in getting any along with us, the drivers having either bolted or been shot down for refusing to bring the beasts on. As we were riding along, we came up with a man walking quietly along the road covered with a blanket. One of the officers was going to kill him, when General Outram said, "Oh do not, he is only a villager:" so the officer pulled the blanket off the man, and exposed a full blown sepoy, musket, belts, and all, of the Oudh Police. You may be sure he did not escape to tell the tale. As I said, we got two guns, limbers and all, and having yoked bullocks to them, off we started back to our force, where you may be sure we were hailed with delight. We met them at Onao, and having halted there for half an hour, got our tots, and some roasted Indian corn, and off we went again, feeling as jolly as possible. We advanced on to, and right through, our *ultima Thule* of the former advance, Busseerut Gunge, and encamped in and about it for the night. Next morning we marched again—having to pass through the dreaded Nawabganj, which on the former occasion had always been held up to us as something very dreadful. However this time we passed through it quite safely—not a soul being seen in the village. On on we went towards Bunnee, wondering whether we should find the bridge broken and the enemy there. At last the bridge came in sight, and on either side what looked very like embrazures; but no guns belched forth on us. On we went, crossed the bridge, entered the village, passed through the village, no one! Our advanced men suddenly made signs of enemy, so up we galloped, and saw a number of Sepoys bolting out of a house. They were too quick for us, and we only killed a few of them: but we succeeded in taking all their kits, among which I found the leave chit of a Sepoy of the 22nd Bengal Native Infantry. Two Commissions of Bombay Native officers were also found there. What a day this was—pouring with rain in torrents, so that often we could not see 50 yards ahead of us. Most fortunately a kind friend at Calcutta had sent me a water-proof coat, which kept me dry—no small thing on these occasions, as you are often unable to get a change, and have, as we had this time, to sleep in the clothes we had on. Such a night too—no tents and no cover of any sort, the rain pouring in torrents:—so you may fancy how jolly we were.

You, who are comfortable in your homes, and read of the gallant deeds of the army little know what the poor soldier has to go through. To him, we officers owe all the honors we get:—but how little this is thought of, when at a well spread board, healths are proposed and speeches made, and General This and Captain That are praised to the sky for gallant deeds: yet it is the poor Private, through whom all this has been done. We forget our Privates too much on these occasions, and with some few, but glorious exceptions, are too prone to take all the credit, as if we had done it all ourselves. At dark that evening we fired a salute of

21 guns from the 24-pounders to give notice to our friends in Lucknow that we were coming, and during the night several fancied they heard a return salute: but this turned out to be a mistake, as the garrison in Lucknow had not heard our guns. Well do I remember that evening, when, looking in the direction of Lucknow, we heard the fire of guns every now and then. How anxiously we talked over the meeting with well known faces, the joy we should be received with, and the certainty that there were some still left, as proved by the firing we heard. It was indeed a time of anxious pleasure, after so many trials to be at last within fourteen miles of our gallant fellow countrymen—a most pleasurable feeling, mixed though it was with a tinge of grief, knowing as we did that many must have been cut off during the time they had been shut up. Next morning the 23rd, we had breakfast in the open air (the rain having cleared off), and marched about 9 o'clock. When we had got about five miles I was sent back with half the Europeans and half the Native Cavalry to protect the baggage, as the enemy's sowars were seen hovering about our flanks. This was rather unfortunate for me; for a soldier always wishes to be to the front. However, back I went, and pulled up under a tope of trees about half way down the line of baggage, which extended I should think two miles along the road; and, having thrown out my videttes, we dismounted to smoke. We had not been long seated, when up came a couple of men with baskets of cakes of all sorts, fresh from Cawnpore. I at once seized on them all, and gave them to the men, as I think a soldier on service ought to eat whenever he can, as he never knows when he may be able to get his next meal. About the same time up came a man with what the soldiers call pop (ginger beer), which we likewise bought; so we had a very fine tiffin. When the last of the baggage had passed us, we mounted and rode along the line till we got about half way to the front, and then we pulled up again; and so on till we arrived on our ground. All this time our forces had not been idle. A battle had been fought, which, as I was not there, I can't describe, but which ended as all the others have done, in our taking

several guns and licking the rebels out of the field. The fight lasted till dark, and the firing appeared to us behind very heavy. When our services could be spared from the baggage, we rode on to the front; and the first man we met gave us the glad tidings of the fall of Delhi, or of that part of it which so commanded the rest of the city, that no doubt remained as to the speedy completion of that business. Our usual luck attended us. No one was hurt, though several had narrow escapes; one man got a graze on the head, another on the leg, from grape. We got up just at dark: the rain had commenced again to pour in torrents, and the country, which was very flat, soon bore the appearance of a wide swamp. Where ever we turned, the water was up to the ankles. How to pitch tents and make the men comfortable was the difficulty. First of all I had to find the tents, which were carried on elephants: but in a pitch dark night, among about 150 elephants, it was no easy matter to find one's own, especially as every one was howling and screaming as loud as he could. Perseverance at last succeeded; and I found the beasts, and at length got our men and ourselves under cover, though the ground inside the tents was not particularly dry. But that was not the worst part of it. We could get nothing to eat, and no fires could possibly be lighted: so we had to content ourselves with dry biscuit and the never failing tot of rum. However, we tumbled to sleep, hoping that to-morrow would see our toils at an end and our brethren in Lucknow relieved from their troubles. Morning broke—a fine day: the camp was regularly pitched, and we found we were not going on that day: so we set to work to get our kits dried, which were all pretty well soaking. Suddenly about 11 o'clock we heard cries of, "The Cavalry are wanted immediately to the rear. The enemy are attacking the baggage." We were not long in getting into our saddles, and, having been joined by the staunch 12th Irregulars, off we went; but we were too late. The enemy's Cavalry had come down among the baggage, and, having at first been mistaken for our own Native Cavalry, had got well amongst our men before the alarm was given. They succeeded in killing some seven or eight of our men and one officer; but they left 17 of their number dead on the road, and then had to fly. While they were riding down the line of baggage, they came upon some 19 prisoners who had been taken, who called out to be released: the sowars passed the word down to some Infantry, who were supporting them, and they advanced and succeeded in releasing them. So much for taking prisoners, and so much for having staunch Native Cavalry with us, who are constantly getting us into trouble one way or another. I can safely say I have never seen them do a single thing yet for our good: they always appear to me to be looking out for the first opportunity to bolt. Well, we got up to the scene of action: a company of rifles was moved forward and two of Olphert's horse guns, with which we advanced; and after giving the enemy some few rounds, which soon sent them, green standard and all, to the right about, we returned and had a quiet day of it.

The morning of the 25th September, 1857, at last arrived. Ever memorable will that day be, for although no great despatch was written about it, the results of that day's fighting, though at so great a cost, may well be looked back to with pride, not only by those engaged, but by the whole of the British Army: for a handful of Europeans forced their way through a densely populated city, every house of which was loop-holed, and filled with an enemy thirsting for their blood. Had there not been a great end to gain, this deed might have been put down as one of the most rash ever undertaken by a General: but knowing as our Generals did the imminent danger our fellow-countrymen and women were in, it was a deed of which we may well all be proud. Early in the morning orders were given to send the whole of the sick and wounded, and all baggage and camp-followers, into the Alum Bagh. This Alum Bagh was a large garden surrounded by a high wall; in the middle of the garden stood a large house, and the entrance to the garden was through a large archway. The force was told to take nothing with them but their rations in their haversacks, and the commissariat to take two days' rations. We were all soon formed up; and about 10 o'clock the first Brigade, headed by General Outram, advanced. The firing from the enemy at once commenced, and for some time was kept up with much spirit. They had guns so placed that they regularly raked our force while advancing: but notwithstanding this heavy fire, our men steadily pushed on, and gradually the enemy's fire slackened and receded. The second Brigade also advanced on the left; and, as usual, our brave troops carried every thing before them. We were kept behind to-day in the rear guard—the first time we were not in the advance. While standing under some trees waiting for the order to advance, one of the enemy's round shot came crashing in amongst us, and struck the bough of a tree just over the head of one of our men, who was lighting his pipe: the man never moved; he did not even cease lighting his pipe, but turned his head up to see where the ball had struck the tree:—it was one of the coolest things I have seen. At last the order was given, "threes right," "advance by sections of threes," "walk, march:" and off we went. Little did any of us think what we had to go through;—we were all pretty new to street-fighting. We went on slowly, and, as we advanced, many a poor fellow was taken back past us in a dooly, and here and there we passed the bodies of our own soldiers, as well as of the enemy, telling too plainly what the fighting had been. We advanced without any interruption till we arrived at the Char Bagh, a very large garden surrounded by a high loop-holed wall, just on the outskirts of the city. As we rode along, our heads and shoulders appeared just over the wall, giving a very good mark for the enemy, who were there waiting for us. They opened upon us; and, I am sorry to say, one of our young Volunteers, by name Erskine, was shot in the side. He was one of three young fellows, who came all the way from Calcutta to join us. Poor boy, well he did his duty! He died three or four days before we got out of Lucknow. He leaves a widowed mother in Calcutta to grieve for him. I hope the Government will do something to shew that they appreciate the services of her gallant boy, who gave his life for them in their time of greatest need. We were ordered to dismount and walk, and thus were completely covered from the fire of the enemy. As we got up to the bridge over the canal, we came across more and more dead and wounded. Here was the place where the Madras Fusiliers so gallantly charged and took the enemy's guns placed in position at the head of the bridge; and in this charge it was we lost so many of our officers and men. When we came up, we found a house just across the bridge occupied by the gallant 78th Highlanders. The remainder of the force had turned down to the right, and proceeded along the banks of the canal, so as to avoid going right through the city. The baggage (what little there was,) and doolies bearing their loads of wounded men, were moving on as fast as possible: but the road was bad, and some of the ammunition carts had stuck: so, we were told to advance and go past them; which we did till we came to some brick kilns, where we found young Havelock, Deputy Adjutant General, with a few rifle men standing on the top of a high mound of broken bricks and rubbish. Here we were ordered to halt and dismount till the whole of the wounded and baggage had passed us. The enemy, seeing a number of us standing on this mound, commenced to fire on us with their rifles, and succeeded in wounding one of the men. At first we thought it must be our own men firing on us by mistake, as the whiz of the bullets sounded very like that of the Enfield: but we soon found out our mistake. The enemy were round us like a swarm of bees. Gradually all the carts and doolies passed us, and there remained only one cart behind. It was loaded with round shot, and had stuck in the road, so that it was impossible to move it. Every exertion was made, but without avail, and we were losing men so fast from the fire of the enemy, who seemed to concentrate their fire on this unfortunate cart, that we were ordered to leave it. During all this time the Highlanders had not been idle. Surrounded as they were by thousands of the enemy, they had to do their best to keep down their fire till the whole of the baggage had passed.

The rebels, finding they could not dislodge them, sent out fresh troops and two guns to try and turn them out. Our gallant Highlanders charged these guns through a withering fire, and succeeded in spiking them: but in doing this they had three officers and thirty men placed *hors de combat*. All the baggage having passed on, they were ordered to follow. They passed us, while, with a Company of the 90th, we were doing our best to keep the rebels back from the kilns. At this time a troop of ours was ordered back, (why, no one can tell: as Cavalry in a narrow road with the enemy lining the hedges is not of much use). But back we went, and there we lost two men shot dead and Lieutenant Lynch wounded severely. I was standing looking down the road by one of the kilns, when bang went a musket out of a house on my right, and whiz came a bullet right across my throat, and killed a man standing on my left. I had a narrow escape,—as it was, the skin of my throat was only slightly cut. All having passed, we were now ordered to move on. We had no sooner turned our backs on the enemy, than they swarmed round us like ants: every house and hedge belched forth its deadly fire. On, on we went, passing dead bodies of horses and men, and the guns, which had been taken, spiked and left behind. At last we got into the broad street leading up to the Tarah Kotee (Observatory) where the Deputy Commissioner's *Kacheri* used to be held. As we went along, no one knowing whether we were taking the right road or not (we had *not*, as it turned out, though it led us to the advance part of our force), we were every where met on all sides by such a fire as I hope I may never see again. How many men were knocked over I cannot say: but I know that nearly every one of our horses carried two men that day, for as a man was wounded he was immediately put up behind one of us. Many of these poor fellows were again hit and knocked off the horses. On, on we went, the Infantry officers gallantly leading their men, rushing first at one house and then at another, and oh! how many a poor fellow was killed—hit in the back. The 78th, who, when they had passed us at the brick kilns had pulled up for us again, lost on this day, I believe, 120 or 130 men. At last we got to the corner of the Tarah Kotee compound, just opposite a large gateway leading into the Kaisarbagh or Chief Palace of the Royal family of Oudh; and here we had to pass so close to the houses, that the enemy, who were in hundreds on the tops, actually flung stones down on the top of us, and spat on us, as we passed. One of our young fellows was knocked down and badly hurt by a stone thus thrown at him. Just as we arrived at this corner, we were delighted to see the blue bonnets of the 1st Madras Fusiliers, several of whom, on seeing us coming, had rushed out to try and keep down the fire of the enemy in the houses; and we saw our own Sikhs coming along a road to our right. It turned out that, instead of following the main body, we had turned up the broad street to the left past the Tara Kotee, instead of going on as they did towards the river and passing the Tara Kotee to the right. When we got up to where our men were, we found them Infantry, Artillery, Cavalry, doolies, and camels—all huddled together in a small square space, just outside the wall of the Ferad Bux Palace, close down by the river Goomtee: and there we remained for an hour and a half, the enemy every now and then firing round shot at us from one of the guns we had spiked and left behind us, and from another they had on the opposite side of the river. Fortunately they fired too high; and so the balls went over our heads, and probably in among their own people. At last the order was given for the advance—the 78th in front this time, and we in the rear. It was now night, and as we passed through the streets, we found them quite deserted: but the fighting had been severe. It was here that General Neill was killed. We got into the garden of the Tara Kotee, where we were obliged to halt, as the guns were all pulled up by the ditches, which had been cut across the streets:—at last, about 2 o'clock, we got into the entrenchment, and so ended this memorable 25th September, 1857.

When we came to count our numbers, we found we had 75 men fit for duty out of 110. Next day we had to get our heavy guns in, which had been left at Martin's house, with the 90th to guard them: and, in getting them in, we suffered very heavy loss from the enemy, who at first had retired, but had returned in great numbers. Major Cooper and Lieutenant Crump here met their death: and here it was where so many acts of gallantry were displayed by our soldiers. One man, Ryan, of the 1st Madras Fusiliers, refused to leave the wounded, who were in a house surrounded by the enemy; and kept up, with some two or three other men, such a fire that the enemy could not effect their purpose of getting into the house to murder the wounded. For this Ryan is to get the Victoria Cross. Here also other men in equally small numbers defended themselves till burned out by the enemy: and here one of the 5th Fusiliers was by mistake left asleep, when the rest of the men were withdrawn. When he awoke in broad daylight, he found himself alone and surrounded by the enemy:—but nothing daunted he cried out, "Come on, my lads; here are the *saipoys!*" and, rushing out, cut his way right through them. We lost on this day thirty one officers and 541 men, out of 2,500 of all ranks; which will give an idea of what the fighting must have been.

We were now within the Bailly Guard, and there was no use in mincing matters—we were in for it. As Cavalry, we were of course useless: but our horses had to be fed, and the Commissariat Department were unable to give them any grain: so all we could do was to get grass; and this, surrounded as we were by the rebels, was no easy matter. Our grass-cutters had to go out for it during the night, and, poor fellows, many of them never returned. Every day, I had men brought to me either shot dead, or wounded, in endeavouring to get grass for our horses; and my heart smote me whenever I had to order them out, as I knew it was to almost certain death. Why they did not desert us I cannot imagine—as inside with us they had barely sufficient to keep them alive, with the chance of being killed or wounded every night. Our horses of course gradually fell off: several died of starvation; numbers were shot by order; and a great many were killed by the enemy's shot and shell, which used to come in pretty thick now and then;—so that, when we did get out of Lucknow, out of a hundred horses we took in, we had about fifty-two to take out with us—and these so miserably thin that few of them could be ridden. On the evening of the third day after we got into the Bailly Guard, the Volunteer Cavalry got orders to hold themselves in readiness to move during the night: and about 10 o'clock about fifty of the Volunteer Cavalry (all we could muster) with all the native Cavalry started under Captain Barrow, with Lieutenant Harding to shew the way, with the intention, I believe, of endeavouring to cut our way through the enemy to Alum Bagh. Had we succeeded in getting out we should have been of great use to the little garrison there, and have relieved the Lucknow Commissariat of so many mouths requiring to be filled. We started. How many of us were to get through had to be proved, though we all felt it would not be many. It was a bright moonlight night: the enemy consequently could see our every movement. We were ordered to keep along the bank of the river for some way; but before we had gone far, we were met by such a heavy fire from the other side, and right in front, that our leaders deemed it prudent to pull up. The whole camp of the enemy was on the alert. Bugles blew, drums beat and sepoys howled. We had two horses wounded, and two men hit; though not much hurt. One man was saved by having two biscuits in his pocket, which turned the ball. We returned—and how thankful we were, I leave to the imagination: for we all felt how desperate was the undertaking.

As we were of no use as Cavalry inside the entrenchments, we had a post assigned to us, known as Innes' post, close to the Church—one of the most exposed posts of the works. The enemy were constantly peppering into it with round shot and shell, and no one dared shew his face any where, but whiz came a bullet past it. We had several men shot there—a number of them hit in the hand. One of our Volunteer Officers,

Lieutenant Hearsay, was very fond of going potting at the enemy; and, always after firing, he used to look to see the effect of his shot. He had often been warned that, while he was looking at one enemy, there were three or four looking at him: but he never would take the advice given him, till one day, while peering about to see what damage he had done, whiz came a bullet, and wounded him in two places in the arm. Poor fellow, it was fortunately only a flesh-wound: but instead of getting any pity, every one burst out laughing. It was a great shame; but he came in looking the picture of misery, and holding up his arm in such a funny way, we could not help it. He has gone down to Calcutta, and, I am glad to say, is doing very well.

One day while we were sitting at breakfast at Innes's post, bang came a 24-pound shot right through the roof, and very nearly fell on one of the men who was lying down, covering us with dust at the same time. We jumped up, and found out that it was one of our own 24-pounders, which we had been firing at some building over our house; but, through the bad practice of the officer firing, it had hit us by mistake; so we sent him up the ball with our compliments, and a request to fire a little higher next time. The enemy were all along the south and west sides of the intrenchments, within (in some places) fifty yards of us; and their constant practice was to make false attacks almost every night. These attacks used to commence with a tremendous fire of musketry, followed by heavy cannonading and loud shouting. At first we used to imagine that they were really coming on: but we very soon found out what it was, and hardly deigned to notice them. Not a shot used to be fired by us: for our men had received strict orders not to fire, unless they saw the enemy—which they seldom did, as they used to sit behind loopholed walls, and blaze away as fast as they could, up in the air, or any where, without taking any particular aim, except that the bullet should fall within the Residency. The consequence was that, although few men were hit while at their posts on the walls, numbers were knocked over by the bullets and cannon shot, which used to be flying all day and night in all directions. No place was quite safe: bullets used to come into the most out-of-the-way places. Men used to be hit, while lying in bed, or sitting down to dinner, inside the houses. One officer, while alseep, had his pillow torn from under his head by a round shot; and a lady, who was sitting outside her door, safe as she thought, had the chair carried away from under her. Notwithstanding all this it is wonderful how few were killed and wounded. Children used to play about, and women and men were constantly walking about, so accustomed to the whiz of the bullets that they never paid any attention to them. It certainly was a dreadful thing to see a cannon ball come rushing through a number of men and horses. I have seen two horses, one tattoo and three men, killed by one shot; and I remember on another occasion seeing the top of a man's head taken off, while cleaning his horse—the ball killing the horse and another next to it. The suddenness with which this happens impresses one very much: you may see it a hundred times, and I think the hundred and first time you would have the same feeling—a feeling of awe at the nearness of death.

The rebels were very short of shell and shot:—the latter they got by picking up what we fired at them, or by beating iron into something like shot, and now and then they used to send any odd thing they could get. Once they sent a smoothing iron. They were most persevering. We had taken most of their large guns from them; but instead they had countless small guns, carrying a ball of 2 or 3lbs. These little guns they used to place on the tops of houses, or any where else, where they had a good command of us; and certainly they did annoy us considerably. Often, after they had fired three or four rounds, one of our large 18 or 24-pounders would open upon them:—but immediately the smoke from our gun had cleared away, out would pop the little gun, and, as, if in defiance, belch forth in its shrill broken voice another round. It was of no use wasting shot on them:—they used I believe to do this merely to draw some of our round shot out of us, of which they were much in want. But their shells were the most extraordinary things:—now and then when our shells, which we threw at them, failed to burst, they used to send them back again: but otherwise they had no 8 inch shells, though they had the mortars: so they used to make up shells of two small hand grenades, round which they used to put tow filled with powder. The consequence was, that when these things fell among us, there were always two reports—the first that of the tow round the hand grenades, which exploded and burst, so leaving the grenade free—and then the second explosion of the grenade itself. At first before we discovered this, we were near coming to grief, as when the first explosion had taken place, we thought all was over, and so used to rise up and perhaps rush to the spot. Then again the rebels used to make stone shells, which never did much damage; and now and then you would hear something coming singing through the air, like a small barrel organ or a large Humming bird:—"hoo, woo, woo, woo, woo, woo, thud,"—it would fall close to you, and you'd find a large block of wood about two feet, or 2½ feet, long and a foot thick. I remember, one morning, while talking to a friend of mine not in the army, seeing something coming through the air in our direction, which burst high up, and did no damage: but it was the most extraordinary thing in the shape of a war-like missile I have seen. When it burst, four or five things flew out of it in different directions, and went whizzing about like one of those English crackers we used to have at home:—but what amused me so much at the time was my friend's face and the way he went dodging and wheeling about, trying to escape from each individual piece which he imagined was coming after him: and when he returned to where I was standing—his face red and warm-looking, and panting with exercise—I thought I should have died with laughing.

We had been in the intrenchments about three weeks, when the news were whispered, "To-morrow only half rations." Living on full rations is hard enough, when you are suddenly brought down to it without rum or liquor of any sort:—but to be reduced to ½lb. meat, ½lb. wheat, ½oz. salt and a pinch of rice, was rather unpleasant to think of. When the time came, we (who had been long in India) did not feel it so much as the Regiments who had just come out from England—men with appetites like horses: but, poor fellows, it could not be helped; and I think those who were not wounded owe their health to their not being able to get too much to eat or any spirits to drink. The people, who felt it, were the sick and wounded. For them there were no comforts—nothing but the hard beef and coarse chupatties: and when the little stock of rum and beer, that was kept for the hospital, was expended, they were indeed badly off. Many a man sunk into the grave for want of stimulants: hardly a single case of amputation ever succeeded; and I do not think there is more than one (a drummer boy in H. M.'s 32d,) who lost leg or arm and lived. Many men died from mere scratches—the slightest almost to a certainty proving fatal: hospital gangrene invariably supervened, and the patient after great suffering died. Poor Major Stevenson of the 1st Madras Fusiliers was hit by a spent ball on the pit of his stomach. He had a kummerbund on at the time; so that the skin was not even raised, and still in a few days it turned into a sore, became gangrenous, and the Major died. Then scurvy broke out; and indeed the hospitals were a melancholy sight. Every thing that could be done by the Medical Officers, was done; but. without medicines or means of any sort, it was hard to fight against disease. The two Generals used to be constantly among the sick, holding out hopes of speedy relief, and doing their best to make the men comfortable. There were others also, who did their utmost to relieve the sufferings of the brave men, who had fought for them. I have seen fair and delicately nurtured ladies, when bullets were flying about like hail, when round shot and shell were common visitors in their houses, when many of them were bereft of husband, children, brothers, and all that they held dear, rise above their own misfortunes, and devote themselves to works of charity and love. When rations had been reduced as low as they could be (and women's rations at the full are much less than those allowed men), I have seen them taking from their own small shares of flour and tea, making delicate chupatties with their own hands; regardless of the bullets, carrying them to the sick and wounded in hospital; and, lest their hair should fall down and annoy those on whom they were attending, they have cut it off. Above all, I have seen them moving about the sick, holding out promises of love and forgiveness and hope through the blood of our dear Saviour out of that Book which we are, many of us, I am afraid, too apt to neglect in the time of our good fortune and ease. As long as English women are such, so long will English men be only too willing to die for them.

The defence of Lucknow will be handed down in history as one of the most memorable events upon record. A few hundred Englishmen, hampered with women and children equal in numbers to themselves, their sick and wounded daily, almost hourly, increasing, cut off from all communication with friends outside, indeed for some time not knowing whether there were any friends nearer to them than Calcutta, surrounded by a countless host of blood-thirsty enemies, under a ceasless fire of cannon and musketry, (for before the first relief under the late Sir H. Havelock reached Lucknow, the fire was such that no one dared shew a finger out of cover) gallantly held their own; and not one step did the rebels gain upon them. If the natives of India are capable of taking a lesson, they will long remember it, and feel how hopeless any attempt would be to drive the English out of India. In the audacity of their pride, pampered as they have been, lauded up to the skies as they always were, they forgot that, in all the deeds of arms in which they had been engaged, they had always been led by the Europeans. Their thought was, "*We* have conquered the Punjab; *we* have won and held India for the Sirkar; now that we are tired of them, we who have done all this, will turn them out and set up a king of our own colour." But they calculated without their host. They found it very different fighting *against* the despised Feringees; and they have now re-learnt a lesson, which was taught them a century ago by Clive. May they remember it!

No one, who has not seen the Residency at Lucknow, can form any idea of the fire the garrison were under. Houses breached (almost) with musketry were never before heard of in warfare: but so close were the enemy, that they had actually loopholed our own walls, and used to fire in on our garrison through these holes. They had recourse to every sort of expedient to overcome us, but never succeeded. Mining was tried; and, with the command they had of labour, they could sink any number of mines. When we had to countermine, we had no labourers; and officers as well as men had to take their turn in the mine. But British pluck and endurance beat them. They were beaten at every thing. They had our sappers and miners taught by us; they had our artillery men—all these, and countless numbers. We had no labourers, and so few artillery men that they had to run from one battery to another as required. Still we beat them. Of course this continual wear on the energies of the men told after five months' siege. How anxiously we used to look for despatches from Cawnpore, which were brought in to us with the greatest difficulty! How many of our messengers never returned; and how excited every one was at the first newspaper being brought in in a bundle of grass! How well thumbed that paper was! No one, who has not been shut up for months, can realize our feelings. At last the joyful news was spread that the Commander-in-Chief would be at Alum Bagh on the 15th Inst. Then we began to count the days, and then when it did arrive and we heard the firing, how anxiously we watched from the different look-outs to see how our force was advancing. Next day we saw the fighting advancing towards the Dilkhoosha:—then up went the Jack on the Martiniere, and we knew our Chief was so far on his way to us. Next day pounding commenced again; and gradually the smoke advanced, till we saw the British flag waving on the Mess house. We had not been idle these three days: mines had been exploded, sorties made, and positions taken up in advance of our old position; so that when the Mess house was taken, the relieved and relieving forces were close to each other. The Chiefs meet. The relief is complete: and in gallop two men, one Col. Berkeley of H. M.'s 32d Regiment, the other Mr. Cavanagh, the head Clerk in the Chief Commissioner's office, who, three days before, had made his way out of Lucknow right through the enemy's camp to the Commander-in-Chief with despatches from General Outram—one of the most daring feats performed during these troublous times. He will no doubt get his reward: he richly deserves it.

We were relieved. Arrangements were made for taking the women and children, the sick and wounded in safety out of the place:—as it had been decided that Lucknow must be vacated for the present. Five months of hard-fighting and toil, such as had never been undergone before, were thus to be thrown away: and many a man, sick as we all were of the place, would willingly have remained rather than let the rebels get in and exult over their imaginary victory. But that it was a wise step, all must acknowledge. Cawnpore was threatened, and the sick and wounded required a large number of troops to convey them in safety out of Oudh. Finally orders were issued that nothing was to be taken except a small bundle of necessaries; and then commenced the destruction of property, clothes of all sorts, silver, and books—some of these no doubt old friends—and the burning of which caused many a tear: but all felt it was better to destroy them, than to leave them to our cowardly foe to gloat over. On the night of the 22nd, all the women and children and sick and wounded having been sent in safety to the Dilkhoosha, the garrison commenced its evacuation of a place they so well knew to defend, and had so nobly defended. By 3 A. M. the place was empty; and next morning we arrived at Dilkhoosha, where we remained as the Chief's rear-guard during his march to the Alum Bâgh. On the 25th, we marched and reached it; and there we are now, watching the enemy, and the enemy watching us.

I have thus brought my account of what I did and saw down to the 25th November 1857. I have said nothing of the siege before General Havelock's force forced their way into Lucknow.

I have not said much of what we did after we got in, as it was much the same day after day—a continual watching the enemy, something like a cat watching at a hole for a mouse (we being the cat), with, for the first week, a sortie now and then, in order to destroy houses which commanded the intrenchments.

The first thought that strikes one regarding this rebellion is that the general rising of the Bengal Army has been caused by a fear that we were going to interfere in some way with their caste—in fact, that it was entirely a matter of caste. I think it has, and it has not—if that can be understood. I have little doubt that the principal instigators will be found to be Mahommedans, and Mahommedans in power, connected with the King of Delhi and the ex-king of Oudh. There is no doubt that as long as there was a king of Delhi, acknowledged though in ever so small a way, and as long as there remained a Delhi for that king to live in, so long would the Mahommedans all over India hope and pray to see him once more seated in State on the throne. The annexation of Oudh, though I believe a wise and necessary measure, has been no doubt the straw that has broken the camel's back, though in a way we never expected. The sepoys, as a body, had nothing they could justly complain of: and it was imagined that they, above all, would be benefited by the annexation of Oudh, as so many of them are drawn from that province, where their families are tillers of the soil, and that by the orders issued during the settlement many of these men's families would be replaced in possession of their old landed rights;—and so they were. But annexation also affected the sepoys in a way which they did not like. It made all the people of Oudh British subjects equally with themselves. Formerly if they had any grievance, they got an *arzee* signed by their commanding officer, which was sent to the resident: and the mere fact of the applicant being a sepoy of the Sirkar Engréz Bahadoor was sufficient, if the man had any right on his side, to gain his cause. After the annexation he found every man in Oudh, even the poorest, had an equal hearing with himself:—he did not like it, and so, I have no doubt, cried out against annexation. That their prejudices were not interfered with is too well known: for these were allowed to interfere with the discipline of the Bengal army. The sepoys no doubt, and indeed others besides sepoys, thought that we were going to do away with caste. This idea was confined perhaps to the uneducated: but I think we have brought it on ourselves by thinking and talking so much about caste. Had the Bengal sepoy been taught duty first and caste afterwards, we should not have had so many against us. I do not for one instant urge that we ought to hurt their feelings as to caste: but I do strongly urge that every sepoy on enlistment ought to be told that he would have to perform his duty as a soldier notwithstanding his caste. It is so in Madras and Bombay, where there are many men from Oudh, of the very men composing the Bengal army, and you never hear caste named as an excuse for not performing any duty. If the high caste men do not like to enlist with such an understanding, there are numbers of others who will. The plea of caste was a false one, though no doubt it took at the time. That we have, as a nation, been greatly to blame in this matter, no one who thinks on the subject but must see. Caste has been raised above our own religion. Any one might endeavour to make converts, or do what he liked for his faith, except the Christians. "Oh those missionaries!" how often does one hear, "they ought to be turned out of India; they are the cause of this mutiny:"—and indeed I have heard an officer say, that he would place any missionary in jail whom he caught in his district, preaching or trying to make converts; while another officer present, said, "If things had been carried on as they were fifty years ago, this mutiny never would have happened." Thank God things are not as they were. Then no doubt officers did know more of their men, and perhaps were better liked by them: but why? I leave to others to answer. Let us, ere it is too late, mend our ways, lest God in His turn deny us. Though we have gone through much suffering, we have been most graciously preserved—God, even our God, fighting for us. Often in our engagements has that beautiful verse in the Psalms recurred to me;—"If it had not been the Lord who was on our side, now may Israel say: if it had not been the Lord who was on our side, when men rose up against us: then they had swallowed us up quick, when their wrath was kindled against us."

There has been a very apparent difference between the effects of the rebellion in our old Provinces and in Oudh;—in the former there has been much more maltreatment of the Europeans by the villagers than in Oudh, and again they (the villagers) have settled down to their old occupations and resigned themselves to their old rulers (the British) much sooner than the people of Oudh. In the Provinces there were no men of weight or influence, who, however they might have wished it, had the power to assist the Government, or individual Europeans. The whole community was broken up into small brotherhoods. Our system had entirely ruined and almost wiped away the old lords of the country: so that when the sepoys got possession of any district, the villagers found themselves powerless to resist, and unable to protect. That the villainous, and barbarous deeds committed have, with few exceptions, been perpetrated by the Mahommedans there is little doubt: and however guilty the Hindoo soldiery may be, the Hindoos as a race have generally been the people to save and protect the Christian. In Oudh we on annexation systematically set to work to ruin and reduce the gentry and nobility of the country. To the honor of most of the District Officers be it said, they protested to the last against this policy. We were, however, forced to carry it through, with a view, as was stated, of restoring to the real proprietors their rights to the landed property: hoping that by so doing, we should raise up such a body of friends, as would hold the dispossessed men in check. How miserably this failed we all know. That it must have done so, all who studied the matter were convinced; and now we appear surprised, that all these gentry, whom we ill-treated and ruined, should fight against us! So evident was the falsity of the policy, that at the outbreak of the mutiny these very men whom we had so treated were told, that if they would remain faithful and assist the Sirkar, they should be restored to certain of their lands from which we had dispossessed them. With one or two exceptions, these men, the Talookdars of Oudh, have behaved well. Wherever any of the British Officers in Oudh were saved, it was these men who protected them. True they have been in arms against us; but is that to be wondered at? Had we treated them better on annexation, we should have had many of those who are now opposed to us, on our side: and I am sure that even now they would come in had they any hopes of being well treated. If they do declare for us, the work in Oudh will be easy enough. We shall be able to govern the country through them: but without them, it will be no easy matter to get things settled down.

Through the whole of these advances and engagements of General Havelock's small force, the want of Cavalry and horse artillery has been sadly felt. We have taken guns without number, and have always beaten the enemy; but we have never been able to inflict such a punishment on them as to make them remember it. They were always too quick for us. Their flights were certainly marvellous: we never could get up to them. Had we had even one good troop of Cavalry, we should have given them much severer lessons than they received. The only time we had enough Cavalry to do any thing, was, when we crossed the river the second time. At Mungurwarrah the Volunteer Cavalry, about 110 strong, followed them up and took two guns: and it was owing to this that the enemy never stood again till we reached Alum Bâgh:—whereas had we been unable to follow them up as we did, they would, no doubt, have stood both at Nowabgung and Bunnee, at both which places they had evidently intended to make a stand.

And now, before I close, I must say a few words on the Volunteer Cavalry, to which, I am proud to say, I have the honor to belong. On our first starting from Allahabad it consisted of about eighteen men and officers. On the road four more officers joined us; and this was our strength through the whole of the engagements till we crossed the river Ganges the first time, when we were strengthened by the addition of forty men from the different Infantry Regiments; and, while encamped at Mungurwarrah, we were joined by some six or eight Volunteers, some of them officers. I sincerely hope the Government will take some notice of the services performed by those composing the corps, and shew that they appreciate them. New to the country, new to the service, unaccustomed to roughing it, brought up accustomed to every luxury, and led to believe that on their arrival in India they would have the same, these young officers willingly threw themselves into the thick of the work, often without a tent, or cover of any sort to shelter them from the rain, or sun, with bad provisions and hard work. Side by side with the Privates, they took their turn of duty: and side by side with them they fought, were wounded, and some of them died. When we got into Lucknow, and were useless as Cavalry, cheerfully they took the musket, and night and day at one of the most important posts did sentry duty with the men. It must not be imagined that, in saying this, I am blowing my own trumpet. I was fortunate enough to be made an officer at the raising of the corps; therefore I have not had to take the duties of a Private, as these gentlemen had. But I am, and shall ever be, proud to say, I have served with them in the field Well and nobly they did their duty: and if Her Gracious Majesty shall grant us a medal for what we have under God's Providence been able to do, proud may those boys be, when they point to the medal on their breast, and say, "I won this, while serving as a private in the field."

Alum Bágh, 26th March, 1858.

Nominal Roll of officers and gentlemen in the Volunteer Cavalry, Capt. L. Barrow, *Commandant, with their rank in the Corps.*

Capt. Sheehy, H. M.'s 81st, 2nd in Command. *Died at Cawnpore of cholera.*

Lieut. Lynch, H. M.'s 70th, Commanding Troop, succeeded Capt. Sheehy as 2nd in Command. *Wounded.*

Lieut. Grant, 3d Madras Europeans, Adjutant. *Died at Cawnpore of cholera.*

Capt. Thompson, 10th B. N. I. Serjeant, succeeded Lieut. Grant as Adjutant.

Lieut. Swanston, 7th M. N. I. Qr. Master and Commanding Troop. *Wounded.*

Lieut. Palliser, 63d B N. I. Commanding Troop. *Wounded.*

Lieut. Chalmers, 45th B. N. I. Private; promoted to Corporal, and then Serjeant.

Lieut. Ramsay, 17th B. N. I. acting Cornet of Troop.

Lieut. Hearsay, 57th B. N. I. Trooper. *Wounded.*

Lieut. Birch, 1st B. L. C. Trooper. *Wounded.*

Cornet Fergusson, 8th B. L. C. Cornet of Troop. *Wounded.*

Ensign Stewart, 17th B. N. I. Trooper.

Ensign Honorable H. Hare, B. N. I. Trooper.

Ensign Brander, 37th, Trooper. *Wounded.*

Ensign Woodgate, 11th B. N. I. Trooper.

Ensign Pearson, 27th, Trooper.

Lieut. Wild, 40th, Trooper.

Capt. Hicks, 22nd B. N. I. Serjeant.

Bt. Capt. Hicks, 6th B. N. I. Trooper. *Wounded.*

Lieut. Brown, 56th B. N. I. Trooper. *Died of cholera at Cawnpore.*

Civilians.

Mr. Anderson, acting Cornet.

Mr. Bews, Corporal.

Mr. Green, Corporal. *Wounded.*

Mr. R. T. Goldsworthy, Trooper.
Mr. — Goldsworthy, Trooper.
Mr. Tarhy, Trooper.
Mr. Erskine, Trooper. *Killed.*
Mr. O'Brien, Trooper.
Mr. Thomas, Trooper.
Mr. Smith, Trooper.
Mr. Berrill, Trooper.
Mr. Voss, Serjeant.
Mr. Wood, Trooper.
Mr. Woods, Trooper.
Mr. Abbott, Trooper.
Mr. C. Marshall, Trooper. *Wounded.*
Mr. E. Marshall, Trooper.
Mr. Volkers, Trooper. *Wounded.*